P E A C E

CLASSIC READINGS FOR CHRISTMAS

PEACE

STEPHEN J. NICHOLS

Illustrated by Simon Pemberton

ℝ *Reformation Trust* A DIVISION OF LIGONIER MINISTRIES, ORLANDO, FL

PEACE: CLASSIC READINGS FOR CHRISTMAS

———

© 2013 BY *STEPHEN J. NICHOLS*

———

Published by Reformation Trust Publishing

a division of Ligonier Ministries

421 Ligonier Court

Sanford, FL 32771

Ligonier.org   ReformationTrust.com

———

Printed in Willard, Ohio

RR Donnelley & Sons

October 2014

First edition, second printing

———

———

CREATIVE DIRECTION: Metaleap Creative
COVER AND INTERIOR DESIGN: Metaleap Creative
ILLUSTRATIONS: Simon Pemberton

———

All Scripture references are from *The Holy Bible, English Standard Version*®, copyright © 2001 by Crossway Bibles, a publishing ministry of Good News Publishers. Used by permission. All rights reserved.

———

LIBRARY OF CONGRESS CATALOGING-IN-PUBLICATION DATA

Nichols, Stephen J., 1970-

Peace : classic readings for Christmas / Stephen J. Nichols. -- First edition.

pages cm

Includes bibliographical references.

ISBN 978-1-56769-301-0

1. Christmas--Prayers and devotions. I. Title.

BV45.N53 2013

242'.335--dc23

2013021864

For Ben, Ian, and Grace—
Merry Christmas!

CONTENTS

FOREWORD

NO HOLIDAY STIRS THE HEARTS of millions as does Christmas. Indeed Christmas is not celebrated for a single day but usually involves a month's season of celebration and contemplation. We've all heard of the lamentations about the commercialization of Christmas and the secularization of Christmas and even those protests from within the Christian community that Christmas is a pagan holiday that should not even be acknowledged. Nevertheless the significance of this time of celebration refuses to go away. No number of Grinches are sufficient to steal it from our culture and from the Church. That's because it is the day among all days when we celebrate the entrance into this world of our Redeemer. In the final analysis, the celebration of Christmas is not so much about the delivery of a baby but is rather the celebration of the incarnation of God (though that incarnation came by means of the bearing of a baby). That baby's birth is of singular importance and significance for the whole of human history, not only for religious considerations, but it is of cosmic significance because the whole explanation of the meaning of creation is found in His person and in His work. Indeed as the Scriptures teach us this baby who was born, was in His pre-incarnate state, the Creator of the world. He is the One in whom, through whom and by whom all things are made. If we travel the world, particularly to the countries of the West, we see the multiple traditions that have arisen by which Christian people celebrate this moment in time. Each of these traditions gives us something to savor and contemplate about the sweetness of our Savior's incarnation.

This book, *Peace*, brings refreshing and profitable insights into the meaning, purpose and the significance of Christmas. It is a valuable book for all of us to have and read as we contemplate this glorious moment of human history.

— R.C. Sproul
Chairman and Founder of Ligonier Ministries
Sanford, Florida
April 2013

CHAPTER I

PEACE CHILD

WHETHER YOU ARE A CHILD OR NOT, Christmas is the most anticipated time of the year. It is a time for giving in a culture of receiving. It is a time to think of others when we so easily and quickly think of ourselves. It is a time to yearn and long for peace when we are surrounded by war, strife, and conflict. It is a time for family. It is a time to celebrate hope.

Just the mention of Christmas conjures up nostalgic images of bells ringing, chestnuts roasting on an open fire, and the family gliding across a snow-covered bridge in a horse-drawn sleigh on the way to Grandma's. It is a time to dream of things that are not. It is a time to wish for all that is off-kilter to be set right. Christmas is a season full of promise. This is the Christmas imagined, the Christmas of commercials and Thomas Kinkade paintings.

In reality, Christmas can be a time of disappointment. It can be a time when some hopes and dreams go unfulfilled. The tranquil family dinner can sometimes careen into strife and conflict. Presents, sacrificed for and lovingly presented, may elicit only a yawn, or a half-hearted "Thank you." The sweater we thought they would love so much gets put right in the drawer, never to emerge again.

Then there are the lonely hearts. Every Christmas carol, every ad depicting the giving of a diamond necklace or of a red bow-clad Lexus, only pounds out the inexorable loneliness that some people experience at this most wonderful time of the year. Psychologists tell us that people's experience of depression peaks around holidays, especially Christmas. This, sadly, is the Christmas experienced by many. The season that starts off so full of promise may very well end in disappointment.

This gap between all that we hope for in this season and all that we actually experience has led to a quest. Charlie Brown will tell you this is the quest for the real meaning of Christmas.

The goal of the quest may be summed up in the greatest of all the wishes and dreams of the Christmas season: peace on earth. Peace among nations, peace among brothers and sisters, peace with our selves. We give gifts, sing carols, and roast chestnuts—well, maybe we only sing about this and don't actually do it. In any case, we do all these things in the hope of finding peace. But peace always seems to remain elusive.

One of the most remarkable stories of Christmas comes from one of the darkest moments of modern history. World War I ravaged a continent, leaving destruction and debris in its wake. The human cost, well in the millions, staggers us. But from the midst of this dark conflict comes the story of the Christmas Truce of 1914. The Western Front, only a few months into the war, was a deplorable scene of devastation. Perhaps as if to give the combatants one day to breathe again, a truce was called from Christmas Eve through Christmas Day.

As darkness settled over the front like a blanket, the sound of exploding shells and the rat-tat-tat of gunfire faded. Faint carols, in French or English voices on one side and in German voices on the other, rose to fill the silence of the night.

By morning, soldiers, at first hesitantly, began filing out of the maze of trenches into the dreaded and parched soil of No Man's Land. There was more singing. Gifts of rations and cigarettes were exchanged. Family photos were passed around. Soccer balls appeared. Up and down the Western Front, soldiers, who only hours before had been locked in deathly combat, now faced off in soccer games.

For one brief but entirely remarkable day, there was peace on earth. Some have called the Christmas Truce of 1914 "the Miracle on the Western Front."

Anxious to print some good news, The Times of London reported on the events of the Christmas Truce. Soldiers recorded the day in letters home and in diaries. Some of those lines made it to newspapers, while others remained unknown until later brought to light. Here's one such line from the diary of a German infantryman:

> *The English brought a soccer ball from the trenches, and pretty soon a lively game ensued. How marvelously wonderful, yet how strange it was. The English officers felt the same way about it. Thus Christmas, the celebration of Love, managed to bring mortal enemies together as friends for a time.*

"Friends for a time," "the celebration of love," "peace on earth"—this is the meaning of Christmas. But these celebrations, these truces, don't last. After Christmas Day, the soccer balls and the soldiers went back into the trenches. The Christmas carols subsided and the war carried on. And even though World War I eventually ended, a few decades later, Europe's countryside and cities became the field of battle once again, as did Africa and the Pacific, during World War II.

Events like the Christmas Truce are worth celebrating. But they lack something. They lack permanence. Such impermanent peace is what we often find in our quest for the real meaning of Christmas. If we are looking for permanent and ultimate goodwill, love, and peace, we must look beyond our gift-giving, get-togethers, and office parties. We must look to no other place than to a manger.

In the Christian story Go[d]
down from the height[s]
down into humanity; dow[n]
recapitulate in the womb
down to *the very roots and*
But He goes down t[o]
ruined world with Him
stooping lower and lowe[r]
complicated burden. He
disappear under the loa[d]
and marches off with the

lescends to reascend. ¶ He comes down; of absolute being into time and space, further still, if embryologists are right, to ncient and pre-human phases of life; *eabed* of the Nature He has created. come up again and bring the whole One has the picture of a strong man to get himself underneath some great must stoop in order to lift, he must *almost* before he incredibly straightens his back whole mass swaying on his shoulders.

~ *C·S· Lewis*

e must look to a baby born not with fanfare, pomp, and circumstance, but to poor parents in desperate times. Joseph and Mary, and the Baby Jesus for that matter, were real historical figures. But in a way, Joseph and Mary extend beyond themselves, beyond their particular place and time. They represent all of us. We are all poor and living in desperate times. Some of us are better than others at camouflaging it. Nevertheless, we are all poor and desperate, so we all need the promise bound up in that baby.

We are in need of a way out of our poverty of soul and the desperate state of our human condition. We find it in this child lying in a manger, who was and is Jesus Christ, the long-promised Messiah, Seed, Redeemer, and King.

he birth of Jesus so many centuries ago might have been a slightly-out-of-the-ordinary birth. Even in ancient times, stalls didn't typically double as birthing rooms and mangers didn't typically double as cribs for new-born babies. And that newborn baby was very much out of the ordinary. Of course, in some respects, He was perfectly ordinary. He was a human being, a baby. He got hungry. He got thirsty. He got tired. When He was born, He was wrapped in swaddling clothes—the ancient equivalent of Pampers.

An infant. Helpless, hungry, cold, and tired.

To perceive Christmas through its wrapping becomes more difficult with every year.

— E.B. White

*Jesus, Lord, we look to thee,
On this day of thine own
Nativity; Show thyself the
Prince of Peace; Bid our
jarring conflicts cease.*

~ Charles Wesley

Yet, this child was the Son of God incarnate. He was Immanuel, which translated means "God with us." According to the Apostle Paul's account, this infant created all things. This infant created His own manger. And this infant, this King, brings peace on earth, ultimate and permanent peace.

n order to understand the story of Christmas, we have to go back. Not back just a few thousand years to the birth of Jesus, but all the way back, back to our first parents, Adam and Eve. God placed them in the lush and perfect garden of Eden. They had everything they needed. It was perfect. Then they sinned. As a consequence, God banished them. Now Adam and Eve lived under the curse. But as God pronounced the curse, thundering from heaven, He also gave them a promise.

God gave Adam and Eve the promise of a Seed, a Seed who would be born of a woman. That Seed would make all that was wrong, right. He would make all that was broken, whole. This Seed would bring peace and harmony where strife and conflict raged like a storm-tossed sea.

In the Old Testament, the third chapter of the very first book, Genesis, speaks of conflict and enmity. Adam and Eve, who had known only the experience of tranquility, would now be locked in bitter conflict. Even the ground would be a challenge. The prick of thorns would be the constant reminder. As the poets say, nature is red in tooth and claw. Even the promised Seed would enter into this conflict, fighting with the Serpent, the great spoiler. But Genesis 3 promises that the Seed would overcome the Serpent, securing the final victory and ushering in wave after wave of peace.

The Seed, however, would be a long time coming.

dam and Eve had Cain and Abel, and neither turned out to be the Seed. When Cain slew Abel, God gave Adam and Eve Seth, a little grace in a very troubled world. But Seth was not the Seed. More sons followed. Generations came and generations went.

Then Abraham appeared on the world's stage. God called this man from ancient times to make from him and his wife, Sarah, a great new nation that would be a beacon of light to a lost and hopeless world. Again, God made a promise to this couple of a Seed, a son. They thought it was Isaac. But Isaac died.

This story was repeated from generation to generation, building anticipation of the One to come who would make all things right, who would bring peace. A widow named Naomi and her widowed daughter-in-law, Ruth, even entered into this story. They were in desperate circumstances. There were no social nets to catch the fall of such marginalized people in the ancient world.

Without husbands and sons, without rights and means, widows lived from meal to meal. They lived on a thread of hope. Then came Boaz and the classic

What human being could know all the treasures of wisdom and knowledge hidden in Christ and concealed under the poverty of His humanity?

— *Augustine*

Infinite and an infant.
Eternal, yet born of a woman ...
Oh, the wonder of Christmas.

— *Charles Haddon Spurgeon*

story of boy meets girl. Boaz met Ruth and they married. Before long, just as the curtain fell on the biblical story of Ruth, a son, a seed, was born to Ruth. This son would be a restorer of life, a redeemer. But he was only a shadow of the Seed to come. He, too, died.

The son born to Ruth and Boaz was named Obed. Obed had a son named Jesse. Jesse had many sons, and one of them was a shepherd. One time this shepherd grabbed a handful of stones and felled a giant. He faced down lions. He also was quite a musician. To everyone's surprise—even his father's—this son of Jesse, the great-grandson of Ruth and Boaz, was anointed king of Israel.

While David was on the throne, God gave yet another promise directly to him. This was another promise of a son. God said David's son would be king forever and there would be no end to his kingdom. That was God's promise.

Mary was not chosen
being, as she undoubtedly
humility or any other
is God's gracious will to
unremarkable, considered
devout, ordinary working
faith and hoping in her

because of any *human merit*, not even for
was, deeply devout, nor even for her
virtue, but entirely and uniquely because it
ove, to choose, to make great what is lowly,
o be of little value. Mary the tough,
man's wife, living in her Old Testament
Redeemer, becomes the mother of God.

—Dietrich Bonhoeffer

rom the beginning in Genesis and straight on through the centuries chronicled in the pages of the Old Testament, the promise of this Seed rose like dawn breaking through the night. The prophet Isaiah sums up all of these promises and expectations: "For to us a child is born, to us a son is given; and the government shall be upon his shoulder" (Isa. 9:6a).

Finally, the Seed, the promised One, appeared. On a winter's night in the little town of Bethlehem, nestled just south of Jerusalem in the land of Israel, came this child, who would be Savior and King. He was unlike any other son in human history. First, all other sons in human history live and die. This one lived and died, then rose again. And in His rising again, He conquered sin, death, sorrow, and sadness. In the words of an Old Testament prophecy, "He rose with healing in His wings" (Mal. 4:2).

This Seed was also different because while He was fully and truly human, He wasn't only human. We have some explaining to do here. He was the God-man, fully human and fully God. If this leaves you scratching your head and a little baffled, you are in good company. Theologians have wrestled with this for millennia. The Apostle Paul puts it this way: "In Christ, the whole fullness of deity dwells in bodily form" (Col. 2:10). Christ is the God-man, deity and humanity joined together. This is a blessed and glorious mystery.

Because Jesus Christ is the God-man, He can do what all of these other sons

Celebrating Advent means being able to wait.

— Dietrich Bonhoeffer

I heard the bells on Christmas Day

Their old, familiar carols play,

And wild and sweet

The words repeat

Of peace on earth, good-will to men!

—Henry Wadsworth Longfellow

could not. He can bring an end to our sin and misery. He can still the storm-tossed seas, as well as the foaming and frothing of strife and conflict. He can bring in the still, calm waters of peace. He can restore us to the garden from which Adam and Eve were expelled. As the poet John Milton declared, Jesus Christ, our Seed, regains the paradise we lost.

Milton makes another fascinating observation. Christ not only gains the paradise Adam lost, but Mary makes a contrast to Eve. Eve partook of the forbidden fruit, having given in to the temptation of the Serpent. Adam followed, then all of humanity followed. It is fitting then, Milton explains, that the Rescuer of us all would come to us by way of a woman.

Mary can be an awkward figure for Protestants. To put it plainly, Protestants sometimes shy away from giving her attention. She should not be worshiped, to be sure. The views of her held by the Roman Catholic Church have come about from centuries of tradition, not from the pages of Scripture. Nevertheless, we should not exclude her from the story.

In the following pages, you'll read from the Gospel of Luke, chapter 1. A section of verses in this chapter has come to be called "The Magnificat," a Latin word based on Mary's declaration that her soul "magnifies the Lord" (Luke 1:46). Mary, after learning from the angel that she would conceive, as a virgin, and give birth to the long-awaited Messiah, visited her cousin Elizabeth. Elizabeth, too, was carrying a child. Her son would be John the Baptist, a fascinating figure in the pages of the Gospels. God used Elizabeth to help Mary understand these events. Mary offered a hymn of praise, "The Magnificat," in response.

In Mary's hymn of praise to God, she stresses two things, her great need and God's superabundance to meet it. Mary speaks of herself as humble, lowly, and poor. Then she speaks of God as mighty, holy, merciful, and good. We are all Mary. We are all poor, hungry, and in dire need. At the root of that need is sin.

Sin was conceived in a garden, takes root in each and every human heart, and has borne tragic fruit throughout human history. But God is merciful. He gave sons to Adam and Eve. Sin was present and spoiled that relationship, leaving one son dead and one guilt-ridden and on the run. But God was merciful and gave another son, Seth. And God gave more sons, more signs for hope in the promise of the Seed to come who would undo and set right what Adam and Eve did and set wrong. But none of these sons could set it right. None of these sons bore the title "Prince of Peace." God has done this for us by giving His one and only Son. Through this Son, all is set right. Peace has come, for the Prince of Peace has come and reigns.

Jesus Christ, born of Mary, born in Bethlehem, born on Christmas morning, brings permanent and ultimate peace on earth. The peace we all long for is found in Christ.

The Shepherds sing;
and shall I silent be?
My God, no hymn for thee?

— George Herbert

This helpless baby, infant born.
This king robed in human flesh
cries for his mother
and reaches for her breast.
He comes to rule and to save,
to bring peace on earth,
this babe in a manger,
this seed, this birth.

CHAPTER II

THE STORY OF CHRISTMAS

IN THREE ACTS

THE PASSAGES THAT FOLLOW retell this ancient story, the beautiful and true story of the first Christmas. This is a story in three acts. The first act concerns the promise, the expectation of the One to come. Here we find the words of the prophets, words of hope in desperate and dark times. The second act declares the fulfillment, the coming of the Son. Here we find the words of the Gospels and of the New Testament letters, words declaring the birth of the Savior. In the third and final act, we find reflection on this event. We find here the words of an old man named Simeon, the words of Jesus' brother James, of the Apostle John, and the words of the Apostle Paul. All three met Jesus, and all three have a story to tell.

These readings from Scripture begin with Genesis and end with Revelation. In the very center is Christ, like the hub of a wheel. In one respect, every word of the Old Testament anticipates the birth, life, death, and resurrection of Jesus Christ. The Gospels tell His story, and the later New Testament Epistles tell us what His story means. At the center is the story of the birth of a child to the virgin Mary in the town of Bethlehem two thousand years ago.

This Christmas story of promise, fulfillment, and reflection is the most endearing story of all time, captured on canvas, in song, and in verse. Alongside the ancient words from the Bible, artists, composers, and poets display in images and words the meaning of these events. We find here not mere nostalgia. We find here the real meaning of Christmas. We find here the story of the birth of Jesus Christ, Immanuel, God with us. We find here the story of life in the midst of death, peace and harmony in the midst of strife and struggle.

Dietrich Bonhoeffer, in a Christmas sermon delivered in London in 1933, asked, "What does it mean to say such things about the Christ child?" In other words, are these sayings we banter about concerning Christmas and the Christ child mere figures of speech, or, as Bonhoeffer put it, "beautiful, pious legends"? Bonhoeffer then answered his own question:

> *It is not just a figure of speech. It is what we have said: that it is God, the Lord and Creator of all things, who becomes so small here, comes to us in a little corner of the world, unremarkable and hidden away, and wants to meet us and be among us as a helpless, defenseless child—not as*

a game or to charm us, because we find this so touching, but to show us
where and who God really is.

Bonhoeffer then put it rather directly: "The judgment and redemption of the world—that is what is happening here. For it is the Christ child in the manger himself who will bring that judgment and redemption." He ended the sermon with a series of questions, leading off with, "Who among us will celebrate Christmas rightly?" He again answered his own question, saying that the one who celebrates Christmas rightly sees "the glory of God in the lowliness of the child in the manger."

In these passages from Scripture that follow, we see precisely this. Not nostalgia, not sentimentality, not charming stories. Christmas far exceeds wrapping paper, red satin bows, and holiday wishes for good will. In the Christmas story, we see the gravest and most glorious of all realities.

THE STORY OF CHRISTMAS

PROMISE

ACT I

WE FIRST ENCOUNTER the promise of the Seed, the Rescuer who is to come, in Genesis 3.

The Old Testament historians, poets, and prophets use this text as a touchstone as they continue to anticipate the coming of the Seed and as they develop the full contours of this promise.

✧✧✧✧✧✧✧✧✧✧✧✧✧✧✧✧✧✧✧

O come, O come, Emmanuel,
And ransom captive Israel,
That mourns in lonely exile here
Until the Son of God appear.

Rejoice! Rejoice! Emmanuel
Shall come to thee, O Israel.

O come, Thou Wisdom from on high,
Who orders all things mightily;
To us the path of knowledge show,
And teach us in her ways to go.

Rejoice! Rejoice! Emmanuel
Shall come to thee, O Israel.

O come, Thou Rod of Jesse, free
Thine own from Satan's tyranny;
From depths of hell Thy people save,
And give them victory over the grave.

Rejoice! Rejoice! Emmanuel
Shall come to thee, O Israel.

O come, Thou Day-spring, come and cheer
Our spirits by Thine advent here;
Disperse the gloomy clouds of night,
And death's dark shadows put to flight.

Rejoice! Rejoice! Emmanuel
Shall come to thee, O Israel.

✧✧✧✧✧✧✧✧✧✧✧✧✧✧✧✧✧✧✧

THE PROMISE OF THE SEED TO ADAM

GENESIS 3:15

"I will put enmity between you [the Serpent] and the woman, and between your offspring and her offspring; he shall bruise your head, and you shall bruise his heel."

THE PROMISE OF THE SEED TO ABRAM

GENESIS 12:1–3

Now the Lord said to Abram, "Go from your country and your kindred and your father's house to the land that I will show you. And I will make of you a great nation, and I will bless you and make your name great, so that you will be a blessing. I will bless those who bless you, and him who dishonors you I will curse, and in you all the families of the earth shall be blessed."

RUTH AND NAOMI'S REDEEMER

Ruth 4:13~17

o Boaz took Ruth, and she became his wife. And he went in to her, and the Lord gave her conception, and she bore a son. Then the women said to Naomi, "Blessed be the Lord, who has not left you this day without a redeemer, and may his name be renowned in Israel! He shall be to you a restorer of life and a nourisher of your old age, for your daughter-in-law who loves you, who is more to you than seven sons, has given birth to him." Then Naomi took the child and laid him on her lap and became his nurse. And the women of the neighborhood gave him a name, saying, "A son has been born to Naomi." They named him Obed. He was the father of Jesse, the father of David.

THE PROMISE OF THE SEED TO DAVID

2 Samuel 7:8~16

"ow, therefore, thus you shall say to my servant David, 'Thus says the Lord of hosts, I took you from the pasture, from following the sheep, that you should be prince over my people Israel. And I have been with you wherever you went and have cut off all your enemies from before you. And I will make for you a great name, like the name of the great ones of the earth. And I will appoint a place for my people Israel and will plant them, so that they may dwell in their own place and be disturbed no more. And violent men shall afflict them no more, as formerly, from the time that I appointed judges over my people Israel. And I will give you rest from all your enemies. Moreover, the Lord declares to you that the Lord will make you a house. When your days are fulfilled and you lie down with your fathers, I will raise up your offspring after you, who shall come from your body, and I will establish his kingdom. He shall build a house for my name, and I will establish the throne of his kingdom forever. I will be to him a father, and he shall be to me a son. When he commits iniquity, I will discipline him with the rod of men, with the stripes of the sons of men, but my steadfast love will not depart from him, as I took it from Saul, whom I put away from before you. And your house and your kingdom shall be made sure forever before me. Your throne shall be established forever.'"

CHRIST BORN AS KING

Charles H. Spurgeon

very singular thing is this, that Jesus Christ was said to have been "born the king of the Jews." Very few have ever been "born king." Men are born princes, but they are seldom born kings. I do not think you can find an instance in history where any infant was born king. He was the prince of Wales, perhaps, and he had to wait a number of years, till his father died, and then they manufactured him into a king, by putting a crown on his head; and a sacred chrism, and other silly things; but he was not born a king. I remember no one who was born a king except Jesus; and there is emphatic meaning in that verse that we sing:

> *Born thy people to deliver;*
> *Born a child, and yet a king.*

The moment that he came on earth he was a king. He did not wait till his majority that he might take his empire; but as soon as his eye greeted the sunshine he was a king; from the moment that his little hands grasped anything, they grasped a scepter, as soon as his pulse beat, and his blood began to flow, his heart beat royally, and his pulse beat an imperial measure, and his blood flowed in a kingly current. He was born a king.

Born thy people to deliver;
Born a child, and yet a king.

THE REIGN OF THE ANOINTED SON

PSALM 2

◇◇◇◇◇◇◇◇◇◇◇◇◇◇◇◇◇◇◇◇◇◇◇◇◇◇◇

Why do the nations rage
and the peoples plot in vain?

The kings of the earth set themselves,
and the rulers take counsel together,
against the Lord and against his anointed, saying,

"Let us burst their bonds apart
and cast away their cords from us."

He who sits in the heavens laughs;
the Lord holds them in derision.

Then he will speak to them in his wrath,
and terrify them in his fury, saying,

"As for me, I have set my King
on Zion, my holy hill."

I will tell of the decree:

◇◇◇◇◇◇◇◇◇◇◇◇◇◇◇◇◇◇◇◇◇◇◇◇◇◇◇

The Lord said to me, "You are my Son;
today I have begotten you.

Ask of me, and I will make
the nations your heritage,
and the ends of the earth your possession.

You shall break them with a rod of iron
and dash them in pieces like a potter's vessel."

Now therefore, O kings, be wise;
be warned, O rulers of the earth.

Serve the Lord with fear,
and rejoice with trembling.

Kiss the Son,
lest he be angry, and you perish in the way,
for his wrath is quickly kindled.

Blessed are all who take refuge in him.

MARY HAD A BABY

Source Unknown

Mary had a baby, oh, Lord.

Mary had a baby, oh, my Lord.

Mary had a baby, oh, Lord.

People keep a-comin' an' the train
done gone.

What did she name Him? Oh, Lord.

What did she name Him? Oh,
my Lord.

What did she name Him? Oh, Lord.

People keep a-comin' an' the train
done gone.

She named Him Jesus, oh, Lord.

She named Him Jesus, oh,
my Lord.

She named Him Jesus, oh, Lord.

People keep a-comin' an' the train
done gone.

Now where was He born? Oh, Lord.

Where was He born? Oh, my Lord.

Where was He born? Oh, Lord.

People keep a-comin' an' the train
done gone.

Born in a stable, oh, Lord.

Born in a stable, oh, my Lord.

Born in a stable, oh, Lord.

People keep a-comin' an' the train
done gone.

THE PROPHET SPEAKS OF THE SON

Isaiah 9:2~7

The people who walked in darkness

    have seen a great light;

    those who dwelt in a land of deep darkness,

    on them light has shined ...

For to us a child is born,

    to us a son is given;

    and the government shall be upon his shoulder,

    and his name shall be called

Wonderful Counselor, Mighty God,

    Everlasting Father, Prince of Peace.

Of the increase of his government and of peace

    there will be no end,

    on the throne of David and over his kingdom,

    to establish it and to uphold it

    with justice and with righteousness

    from this time forth and forevermore.

The zeal of the Lord of hosts will do this.

The Son of God did
heaven. Therefore he
humility and came
into the womb of his
went on to the cross
on earth so that we

not want to be seen and found in descended from heaven into this to us in our flesh, laid himself mother and into the manger and This was the *ladder* that he placed might ascend to God on it.

~ *Martin Luther on Isaiah 9:6*

CHRIST BORN AS KING

Isaiah 11:1~9

There shall come forth a shoot from the stump of Jesse, and a branch from his roots shall bear fruit. And the Spirit of the Lord shall rest upon him, the Spirit of wisdom and understanding, the Spirit of counsel and might, the Spirit of knowledge and the fear of the Lord.

And his delight shall be in the fear of the Lord. He shall not judge by what his eyes see, or decide disputes by what his ears hear, but with righteousness he shall judge the poor, and decide with equity for the meek of the earth; and he shall strike the earth with the rod of his mouth, and with the breath of his lips he shall kill the wicked. Righteousness shall be the belt of his waist, and faithfulness the belt of his loins.

The wolf shall dwell with the lamb, and the leopard shall lie down with the young goat, and the calf and the lion and the fattened calf together; and a little child shall lead them. The cow and the bear shall graze; their young shall lie down together; and the lion shall eat straw like the ox.

The nursing child shall play over the hole of the cobra, and the weaned child shall put his hand on the adder's den. They shall not hurt or destroy in all my holy mountain; for the earth shall be full of the knowledge of the Lord as the waters cover the sea.

But you, O Bethlehem Ephrathah,
who are too little to be among the
clans of Judah,
from you shall come forth for me
one who is to be ruler in Israel,
whose origin is from of old,
from ancient days.

— Out of Bethlehem, Micah 5:2

Therefore the Lord himself will give you a sign. Behold, the virgin shall conceive and bear a son, and shall call his name Immanuel.

— *Immanuel, God with Us , Isaiah 7:14*

O LITTLE TOWN OF BETHLEHEM

Phillips Brooks, 1868

O little town of Bethlehem,
    how still we see thee lie;
Above thy deep and dreamless
    sleep the silent stars go by:
Yet in thy dark streets shineth
    the everlasting light;
The hopes and fears of all the years
    are met in thee tonight.

How silently, how silently,
    the wondrous gift is given.
So God imparts to human hearts
    the blessings of His heaven.
No ear may hear His coming,
    but in this world of sin,
Where meek souls will receive Him
    still, the dear Christ enters in.

For Christ is born of Mary;
    and gathered all above,
While mortals sleep, the angels keep
    their watch of wondering love.
O morning stars, together proclaim
    the holy birth.
And praises sing to God the King,
    and peace to men on earth.

O holy child of Bethlehem,
    descend to us, we pray;
Cast out our sin and enter in;
    be born in us today.
We hear the Christmas angels
    the great glad tidings tell;
O come to us, abide with us,
    our Lord Emmanuel.

ON THE INCARNATION

Leo the Great

herefore the Word of God, Himself God, the Son of God who in the beginning was with God, through whom all things were made and without whom was nothing made (John 1:1–3), with the purpose of delivering man from eternal death, became man: so bending Himself to take on Him our humility without decrease in His own majesty, that remaining what He was and assuming what He was not, He might unite the true form of a slave to that form in which He is equal to God the Father, and join both natures together by such a compact that the lower should not be swallowed up in its exaltation nor the higher impaired by its new associate. Without detriment therefore to the properties of either substance which then came together in one person, majesty took on humility, strength weakness, eternity mortality: and for the paying off of the debt, belonging to our condition, inviolable nature was united with possible nature, and true God and true man were combined to form one Lord, so that, as suited the needs of our case, one and the same Mediator between God and men, the Man Christ Jesus, could both die with the one and rise again with the other.

THE STORY OF CHRISTMAS

FULFILLMENT

ACT II

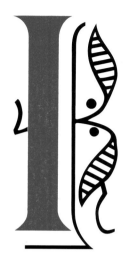

IN ANCIENT TIMES, genealogies revealed a great deal about a person.

A person's identity was bound up in his genealogy. So we learn of Christ's identity through His genealogy. We learn that while He is the son of Mary and Joseph, He is also the son of David, of Jesse, of Obed, of Ruth and Boaz.

He is the son of Abraham, and even, as Luke tells us, the son of Adam.

The gospel writers proceed to reveal even more of the true identity of this baby born in Bethlehem.

EXCERPTS FROM MATTHEW'S GENEALOGY

Matthew 1:1–2, 5–6a, 16

The book of the genealogy of Jesus Christ, the son of David, the son of Abraham. Abraham was the father of Isaac, and Isaac the father of Jacob, and Jacob the father of Judah and his brothers … and Salmon the father of Boaz by Rahab, and Boaz the father of Obed by Ruth, and Obed the father of Jesse, and Jesse the father of David the king … and Jacob the father of Joseph the husband of Mary, of whom Jesus was born, who is called Christ.

EXCERPTS FROM LUKE'S GENEALOGY

Luke 3:23, 31b–32a, 34a, 38

Jesus, when he began his ministry, was about thirty years of age, being the son (as was supposed) of Joseph, the son of Heli … the son of Nathan, the son of David, the son of Jesse, the son of Obed, the son of Boaz … the son of Jacob, the son of Isaac, the son of Abraham … the son of Seth, the son of Adam, the son of God.

MATTHEW'S ACCOUNT OF THE BIRTH

Matthew 1:18~25

ow the birth of Jesus Christ took place in this way. When his mother Mary had been betrothed to Joseph, before they came together she was found to be with child from the Holy Spirit. And her husband Joseph, being a just man and unwilling to put her to shame, resolved to divorce her quietly. But as he considered these things, behold, an angel of the Lord appeared to him in a dream, saying,

"Joseph, son of David, do not fear to take Mary as your wife, for that which is conceived in her is from the Holy Spirit. She will bear a son, and you shall call his name Jesus, for he will save his people from their sins."

All this took place to fulfill what the Lord had spoken by the prophet:

"Behold, the virgin shall conceive and bear a son, and they shall call his name Immanuel" (which means, God with us).

When Joseph woke from sleep, he did as the angel of the Lord commanded him: he took his wife, but knew her not until she had given birth to a son. And he called his name Jesus.

ON THE NATIVITY

John Chrysostom

ow shall I describe this Birth to you? For this wonder fills me with astonishment. The Ancient of days has become an infant. He who sits upon the sublime and heavenly Throne, now lies in a manger. And He who cannot be touched, who is simple, without complexity, and incorporeal, now lies subject to the hands of men. He who has broken the bonds of sinners, is now bound by an infant's bands. But He has decreed that ignominy shall become honor, infamy be clothed with glory, and total humiliation the measure of His Goodness.

For this He assumed my body, that I may become capable of His Word; taking my flesh, He gives me His spirit; and so He bestowing and I receiving, He prepares for me the treasure of Life. He takes my flesh, to sanctify me; He gives me His Spirit, that He may save me.

Come, then, let us observe the Feast. Truly wondrous is the whole chronicle of the Nativity. For this day the ancient slavery is ended, the devil confounded, the demons take to flight, the power of death is broken, paradise is unlocked, the curse is taken away, sin is removed from us, error driven out, truth has been brought back.

MARY'S CALLING, VISIT WITH ELIZABETH, & HER SONG OF PRAISE, "THE MAGNIFICAT"

Luke 1:26~56

n the sixth month the angel Gabriel was sent from God to a city of Galilee named Nazareth, to a virgin betrothed to a man whose name was Joseph, of the house of David. And the virgin's name was Mary. And he came to her and said, "Greetings, O favored one, the Lord is with you!" But she was greatly troubled at the saying, and tried to discern what sort of greeting this might be. And the angel said to her,

"Do not be afraid, Mary, for you have found favor with God. And behold, you will conceive in your womb and bear a son, and you shall call his name Jesus. He will be great and will be called the Son of the Most High. And the Lord God will give to him the throne of his father David, and he will reign over the house of Jacob forever, and of his kingdom there will be no end."

And Mary said to the angel, "How will this be, since I am a virgin?"

And the angel answered her,

"The Holy Spirit will come upon you, and the power of the Most High will overshadow you; therefore the child to be born will be called holy—the Son of God. And behold, your relative Elizabeth in her old age has also conceived a son, and this is the sixth month with her who was called barren. For nothing will be impossible with God."

And Mary said, "Behold, I am the servant of the Lord; let it be to me according to your word." And the angel departed from her.

In those days Mary arose and went with haste into the hill country, to a town in Judah, and she entered the house of Zechariah and greeted Elizabeth. And when Elizabeth heard the greeting of Mary, the baby leaped in her womb. And Elizabeth was filled with the Holy Spirit, and she exclaimed with a loud cry,

"Blessed are you among women, and blessed is the fruit of your womb! And why is this granted to me that the mother of my Lord should come to me? For behold, when the sound of your greeting came to my ears, the baby in my womb leaped for joy. And blessed is she who believed that there would be a fulfillment of what was spoken to her from the Lord." And Mary said,

"My soul magnifies the Lord,
and my spirit rejoices in God my Savior,
for he has looked on the humble estate of his servant.
For behold, from now on all generations will call me blessed;
for he who is mighty has done great things for me,
and holy is his name.

And his mercy is for those who fear him

from generation to generation.

He has shown strength with his arm;

he has scattered the proud in the thoughts of their hearts;

he has brought down the mighty from their thrones

and exalted those of humble estate;

he has filled the hungry with good things,

and the rich he has sent away empty.

He has helped his servant Israel,

in remembrance of his mercy,

as he spoke to our fathers,

to Abraham and to his offspring forever."

And Mary remained with her about three months and returned to her home.

ON KEEPING CHRISTMAS

Augustine

wake, mankind! For your sake God has become man. Awake, you who sleep, rise up from the dead, and Christ will enlighten you. I tell you again: for your sake, God became man.

You would have suffered eternal death, had he not been born in time. Never would you have been freed from sinful flesh, had he not taken on himself the likeness of sinful flesh. You would have suffered everlasting unhappiness, had it not been for this mercy. You would never have returned to life, had he not shared your death. You would have been lost if he had not hastened to your aid. You would have perished, had he not come.

Let us then joyfully celebrate the coming of our salvation and redemption. Let us celebrate the festive day on which he who is the great and eternal day came from the great and endless day of eternity into our own short day of time.

LUKE'S ACCOUNT OF THE BIRTH

LUKE 2:1~7

n those days a decree went out from Caesar Augustus that all the world should be registered. This was the first registration when Quirinius was governor of Syria. And all went to be registered, each to his own town. And Joseph also went up from Galilee, from the town of Nazareth, to Judea, to the city of David, which is called Bethlehem, because he was of the house and lineage of David, to be registered with Mary, his betrothed, who was with child. And while they were there, the time came for her to give birth. And she gave birth to her firstborn son and wrapped him in swaddling cloths and laid him in a manger, because there was no place for them in the inn.

NO ROOM AT THE INN

Martin Luther

 he inn was full. No one would release a room to this pregnant woman. She had to go to a cow stall and there bring forth the Maker of all creatures because nobody would give way. Shame on you, wretched Bethlehem! The inn ought to have been burned with brimstone, for even though Mary had been a beggar maid or unwed, anybody at such a time would have been glad to give her a hand. There are many of you in this congregation who think to yourselves: "If only I had been there! How quick I would have been to help the baby! I would have washed his linen! How happy I would have been to go with the shepherds to see the Lord lying in the manger!" Yes you would! You say that because you know how great Christ is, but if you had been there at that time you would have done no better than the people of Bethlehem. Childish and silly thoughts are these! Why don't you do it now? You have Christ in your neighbor. You ought to serve him, for what you do to your neighbor in need you do to the Lord Christ himself.

THE ANNOUNCEMENT TO THE SHEPHERDS

LUKE 2:8~14

And in the same region there were shepherds out in the field, keeping watch over their flock by night. And an angel of the Lord appeared to them, and the glory of the Lord shone around them, and they were filled with fear. And the angel said to them,

> "Fear not, for behold, I bring you good news of a great joy that will be for all the people. For unto you is born this day in the city of David a Savior, who is Christ the Lord. And this will be a sign for you: you will find a baby wrapped in swaddling cloths and lying in a manger."

And suddenly there was with the angel a multitude of the heavenly host praising God and saying,

> "Glory to God in the highest, and on earth peace among those with whom he is pleased!"

THE SHEPHERDS AND THE BABE

R.C. Sproul

n the night Jesus was born something spectacular took place. The plains of Bethlehem became the theater for one of the most spectacular sound-and-light shows in human history. All heaven broke loose ...

When the shepherds of Bethlehem quaked in fear, they were admonished by the angel: "Do not be afraid, for behold I bring you good tidings of great joy which will be to all people. For there is born to you this day in the city of David a Savior, who is Christ the Lord" (Luke 2:10–11, NKJV).

Every human being longs for a savior of some type. We look for someone or something that will solve our problems, ease our pain, or grant the most elusive goal of all, happiness. From the pursuit of success in business to the discovery of a perfect mate or friend, we make our search ...

The burst of light that flooded the fields of Bethlehem announced the advent of a Savior who was able to do the task.

We note that the newborn Savior is also called "Christ the Lord." To the astonished shepherds these titles were pregnant with meaning. This Savior is the Christ, the long-awaited Messiah of Israel. Every Jew remembered the promise of God that someday the Messiah, the Lord's anointed, would come to deliver

Israel. This Messiah-Savior is also Lord. He not only will save His people but He will be their King, their Sovereign.

The angel declares that this Savior-Messiah-Lord is born "unto you." The divine announcement is not an oracle of judgment but the declaration of a gift. The newborn King is born for us.

Luke 2:15~20

⬦⬦⬦⬦⬦⬦⬦⬦⬦⬦⬦⬦⬦⬦⬦⬦⬦⬦⬦⬦⬦⬦

When the angels went away from them into heaven, the shepherds said to one another, "Let us go over to Bethlehem and see this thing that has happened, which the Lord has made known to us." And they went with haste and found Mary and Joseph, and the baby lying in a manger. And when they saw it, they made known the saying that had been told them concerning this child. And all who heard it wondered at what the shepherds told them. But Mary treasured up all these things, pondering them in her heart. And the shepherds returned, glorifying and praising God for all they had heard and seen, as it had been told them.

⬦⬦⬦⬦⬦⬦⬦⬦⬦⬦⬦⬦⬦⬦⬦⬦⬦⬦⬦⬦⬦⬦

FOR UNTO US

Martin Luther

ehold here what the Gospel is, namely, a joyful sermon concerning Christ, our Savior. Whoever preaches him rightly, preaches the Gospel of pure joy. How is it possible for man to hear of greater joy than that Christ has given to him as his own? He does not only say Christ is born, but he makes his birth our own by saying, to you a Savior.

Therefore the Gospel does not only teach the history concerning Christ; but it enables all who believe it to receive it as their own ... Of what benefit would it be to me if Christ had been born a thousand times, and it would daily be sung into my ears in a most lovely manner, if I were never to hear that he was born for me and was to be my very own? If the voice gives forth this pleasant sound, even if it be in homely phrase, my heart listens with joy for it is a lovely sound which penetrates the soul.

SILENT NIGHT! HOLY NIGHT!

Joseph Mohr, 1818

Silent night! Holy night!
All is calm, all is bright
Round yon virgin mother and child.
Holy infant, so tender and mild,
Sleep in heavenly peace,
Sleep in heavenly peace.

Silent night! Holy night!
Shepherds quake at the sight!
Glories stream from heaven afar,
Heavenly hosts sing alleluia;
Christ, the Savior, is born!
Christ, the Savior, is born!

Silent night! Holy night!
Son of God, love's pure light
Radiant beams from Thy holy face
With the dawn of redeeming grace,
Jesus, Lord, at Thy birth,
Jesus, Lord, at Thy birth.

THE STORY OF CHRISTMAS

REFLECTION

ACT III

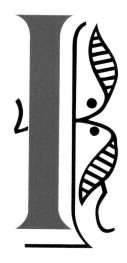

IN THE THIRD AND FINAL ACT, the writers of Scripture

reflect on the meaning and significance of the birth of

Christ. His was no ordinary birth, no ordinary life, and no

ordinary death.

In these reflections, we come to find the ultimate

meaning of Christmas.

JOHN REFLECTS ON THE BIRTH: GOD MADE FLESH

John 1:1~14

In the beginning was the Word, and the Word was with God, and the Word was God. He was in the beginning with God. All things were made through him, and without him was not any thing made that was made. In him was life, and the life was the light of men. The light shines in the darkness, and the darkness has not overcome it.

There was a man sent from God, whose name was John. He came as a witness, to bear witness about the light, that all might believe through him. He was not the light, but came to bear witness about the light.

The true light, which enlightens everyone, was coming into the world. He was in the world, and the world was made through him, yet the world did not know him. He came to his own, and his own people did not receive him. But to all who did receive him, who believed in his name, he gave the right to become children of God, who were born, not of blood nor of the will of the flesh nor of the will of man, but of God.

And the Word became flesh and dwelt among us, and we have seen his glory, glory as of the only Son from the Father, full of grace and truth.

GRACE UPON GRACE

John Piper

hat is the connection between all this revelation and you? Verse 16 gives the answer: "And from his fullness have we all received grace upon grace." ... God came not just to show us grace but to give us grace; and we must receive it.

... This Christmas he wants to treat you with grace—to forgive all your sins—all of them!—to take away all your guilt, to make your conscience clean, to help you with your problems, to give you strength for each day, and to fill you with hope and joy and peace. Isn't that the meaning of grace? And isn't that why he pitched his tent among us?

But note well the word: "From his fullness we have received grace upon grace." Don't spurn it. Receive it. Welcome it for what it really is. And let it fill your heart with everlasting joy—joy to the world!

For God so loved
Son, that whoever
perish but have
send his Son into
world, but in order
through him.

the world, that he gave his only

believes in him should not

ternal life. For God did not

the world to condemn the

that the world might be saved

~ God Sent His Son to Save, John 3:16~17

O COME, ALL YE FAITHFUL

John Francis Wade, 1751

O come, all ye faithful,

Joyful and triumphant,

O come ye, O come ye to Bethlehem;

Come and behold Him

Born the King of angels;

O come, let us adore Him,

O come, let us adore Him,

O come, let us adore Him,

Christ the Lord.

Sing, choirs of angels,

Sing in exultation,

Sing, all ye citizens of heav'n above;

Glory to God

In the highest

O come, let us adore Him,

O come, let us adore Him,

O come, let us adore Him,

Christ the Lord.

SIMEON ENCOUNTERS THE CHILD

LUKE 2:25~32

ow there was a man in Jerusalem, whose name was Simeon, and this man was righteous and devout, waiting for the consolation of Israel, and the Holy Spirit was upon him. And it had been revealed to him by the Holy Spirit that he would not see death before he had seen the Lord's Christ. And he came in the Spirit into the temple, and when the parents brought in the child Jesus, to do for him according to the custom of the Law, he took him up in his arms and blessed God and said,

> "Lord, now you are letting your servant depart in peace,
> according to your word;
> for my eyes have seen your salvation
> that you have prepared in the presence of all peoples,
> a light for revelation to the Gentiles,
> and for glory to your people Israel."

GALATIANS 4:4~7

◇◇◇◇◇◇◇◇◇◇◇◇◇◇◇◇◇◇◇◇◇◇

But when the fullness of time had come, God sent forth his Son, born of woman, born under the law, to redeem those who were under the law, so that we might receive adoption as sons. And because you are sons, God has sent the Spirit of his Son into our hearts, crying, "Abba! Father!" So you are no longer a slave, but a son, and if a son, then an heir through God.

◇◇◇◇◇◇◇◇◇◇◇◇◇◇◇◇◇◇◇◇◇◇

THE HUMILITY OF THE MANGER AND THE CROSS

PHILIPPIANS 2:5~11

ave this mind among yourselves, which is yours in Christ Jesus, who, though he was in the form of God, did not count equality with God a thing to be grasped, but made himself nothing, taking the form of a servant, being born in the likeness of men. And being found in human form, he humbled himself by becoming obedient to the point of death, even death on a cross. Therefore God has highly exalted him and bestowed on him the name that is above every name, so that at the name of Jesus every knee should bow, in heaven and on earth and under the earth, and every tongue confess that Jesus Christ is Lord, to the glory of God the Father.

ON THE FEAST OF CHRISTMAS

Charles H. Spurgeon

e have nearly arrived at the great merry-making season of the year. On Christmas-day we shall find all the world in England enjoying themselves with all the good cheer which they can afford. Servants of God, you who have the largest share in the person of him who was born at Bethlehem, I invite you to the best of all Christmas fare—to nobler food than makes the table groan—bread from heaven, food for your spirit. Behold, how rich and how abundant are the provisions which God has made for the high festival which he would have his servants keep, not now and then, but all the days of their lives!

WHO IS THIS CHILD?

Colossians 1:15~20; 2:9~10

e is the image of the invisible God, the firstborn of all creation. For by him all things were created, in heaven and on earth, visible and invisible, whether thrones or dominions or rulers or authorities—all things were created through him and for him. And he is before all things, and in him all things hold together. And he is the head of the body, the church. He is the beginning, the firstborn from the dead, that in everything he might be preeminent. For in him all the fullness of God was pleased to dwell, and through him to reconcile to himself all things, whether on earth or in heaven, making peace by the blood of his cross.

For in him the whole fullness of deity dwells bodily, and you have been filled in him, who is the head of all rule and authority.

ON CHRIST'S BIRTH AND
THE HOPE OF GLORY AND GRACE

Augustine

 ustified by faith, let us be at peace with God: for justice and peace have embraced one another. Through our Lord Jesus Christ: for Truth has arisen from the earth, through whom we have access to that grace in which we stand, and our boast is in our hope of God's glory ... Therefore he who glories, let him glory, not in himself, but in the Lord.

For this reason, when our Lord was born of the Virgin, the message of the angelic voices was: Glory to God in the highest, and peace to men of good will.

For how could there be peace on earth unless Truth has arisen from the earth, that is, unless Christ were born of our flesh? And he is our peace who made the two into one: that we might be men of good will, sweetly linked by the bond of unity.

Let us then rejoice in this grace, so that our glorying may bear witness to our good conscience by which we glory, not in ourselves, but in the Lord. That is why Scripture says: He is my glory, the one who lifts up my head. For what greater grace could God have made to dawn on us than to make his only Son become the son of man, so that a son of man might in his turn become son of God?

Ask if this were merited; ask for its reason, for its justification, and see whether you will find any other answer but sheer grace.

We have peace with God through our Lord Jesus Christ.

— The Real Meaning of Christmas, Romans 5:1b

JOHN REFLECTS ON THE EXALTATION OF THE LAMB

REVELATION 5:1~14

hen I saw in the right hand of him who was seated on the throne a scroll written within and on the back, sealed with seven seals. And I saw a strong angel proclaiming with a loud voice, "Who is worthy to open the scroll and break its seals?" And no one in heaven or on earth or under the earth was able to open the scroll or to look into it, and I began to weep loudly because no one was found worthy to open the scroll or to look into it. And one of the elders said to me, "Weep no more; behold, the Lion of the tribe of Judah, the Root of David, has conquered, so that he can open the scroll and its seven seals."

And between the throne and the four living creatures and among the elders I saw a Lamb standing, as though it had been slain, with seven horns and with seven eyes, which are the seven spirits of God sent out into all the earth. And he went and took the scroll from the right hand of him who was seated on the throne. And when he had taken the scroll, the four living creatures and the twenty-four elders fell down before the Lamb, each holding a harp, and golden bowls full of incense, which are the prayers of the saints. And they sang a new song, saying,

"Worthy are you to take the scroll

and to open its seals,

for you were slain,

and by your blood you ransomed people for God

from every tribe and language and people and nation,

and you have made them a kingdom

and priests to our God,

and they shall reign on the earth."

Then I looked, and I heard around the throne and the living creatures and the elders the voice of many angels, numbering myriads of myriads and thousands of thousands, saying with a loud voice, "Worthy is the Lamb who was slain, to receive power and wealth and wisdom and might and honor and glory and blessing!" And I heard every creature in heaven and on earth and under the earth and in the sea, and all that is in them, saying, "To him who sits on the throne and to the Lamb be blessing and honor and glory and might forever and ever!" And the four living creatures said, "Amen!" and the elders fell down and worshiped.

ON THE MORNING OF CHRIST'S NATIVITY (FIRST STANZA)

John Milton

⬦⬦⬦⬦⬦⬦⬦⬦⬦⬦⬦⬦⬦⬦⬦⬦⬦

This is the month,
and this the happy morn

Wherein the Son of
Heav'n's eternal King,

Of wedded Maid,
and Virgin Mother born,

Our great redemption
from above did bring;

For so the holy sages
once did sing,

That He our deadly
forfeit should release,

And with His Father work
us a perpetual peace.

⬦⬦⬦⬦⬦⬦⬦⬦⬦⬦⬦⬦⬦⬦⬦⬦⬦⬦⬦⬦

JOHN REFLECTS ON THE CHIEF END OF THE FIRST CHRISTMAS

REVELATION 21:1~5

hen I saw a new heaven and a new earth, for the first heaven and the first earth had passed away, and the sea was no more. And I saw the holy city, new Jerusalem, coming down out of heaven from God, prepared as a bride adorned for her husband. And I heard a loud voice from the throne saying, "Behold, the dwelling place of God is with man. He will dwell with them, and they will be his people, and God himself will be with them as their God. He will wipe away every tear from their eyes, and death shall be no more, neither shall there be mourning, nor crying, nor pain anymore, for the former things have passed away."

And he who was seated on the throne said, "Behold, I am making all things new." Also he said, "Write this down, for these words are trustworthy and true."

CHAPTER III

THE GIFT OF PEACE

THE STORY OF CHRISTMAS is the story of the birth of the Savior. The long-awaited Seed has come. The promise has been fulfilled. Unto us a Son is given. Jesus came to bring one gift, the gift of salvation. The Apostle Paul summed it up as well as anyone possibly could. Because Christ came, because He lived, because He died, because He rose again, we have peace with God (Rom. 5:1b). We have forgiveness. We have been granted full access to the Father and to His grace.

The birthday of the Lord is the birthday of Peace.

—Leo I, "On the Feast of the Nativity"

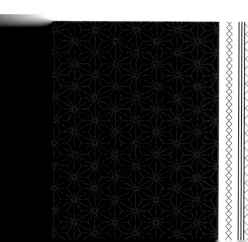

ecause we have peace with God, we can also have peace with one another. We can sing of and long for peace on earth, for someday another of God's promises will be fulfilled. This promise, too, concerns Christ. This promise entails the full and uninhibited reign of Christ, the Lamb, on the throne.

Christmas ultimately tells the story of a journey. It is the journey of Christ from the heights of heaven to a lowly place on earth, from the glory of heaven to a humble manger. From there, Christ's journey took Him to a cross, and then to a tomb. But His journey did not end there, for He rose victoriously. Then He ascended back to the heavens. Someday He will come again. God has promised, and we know God keeps His promises.

May you have a truly blessed Christmas as you celebrate and share the good news of our Savior's birth.

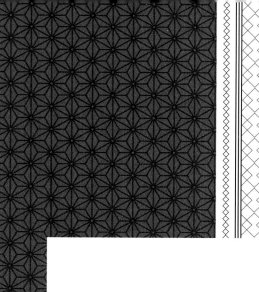

For unto you is born this day in the city of David a Savior, who is Christ the Lord.

—Luke 2:11

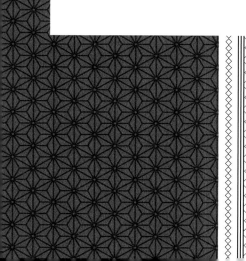

GO, TELL IT ON THE MOUNTAIN

Source Unknown

◇◇◇◇◇◇◇◇◇◇◇◇◇◇◇◇◇◇◇◇◇◇◇◇◇◇◇◇◇◇◇◇◇◇

Go, tell it on the mountain,
Over the hills and everywhere;
Go, tell it on the mountain
That Jesus Christ is born.

While shepherds kept their watching
O'er silent flocks by night,
Behold throughout the heavens
There shone a holy light.

Go, tell it on the mountain,
Over the hills and everywhere;
Go, tell it on the mountain
That Jesus Christ is born.

The shepherds feared and trembled
When, lo! above the earth
Rang out the angel chorus
That hailed our Savior's birth.

Go, tell it on the mountain,
Over the hills and everywhere;
Go, tell it on the mountain
That Jesus Christ is born.

◇◇◇◇◇◇◇◇◇◇◇◇◇◇◇◇◇◇◇◇◇◇◇◇◇◇◇◇◇◇◇◇◇◇

Down in a lowly manger
Our humble Christ was born,
And God sent us salvation
that blessed Christmas morn.

Go, tell it on the mountain,
Over the hills and everywhere;
Go, tell it on the mountain
That Jesus Christ is born.

When I was a seeker
I sought both night and day;
I sought the Lord to help me,
And He showed me the way.

Go, tell it on the mountain,
Over the hills and everywhere;
Go, tell it on the mountain
That Jesus Christ is born.

He made me a watchman
Upon the city wall,
And if I am a Christian,
I am the least of all.

Go, tell it on the mountain,
Over the hills and everywhere;
Go, tell it on the mountain
That Jesus Christ is born.

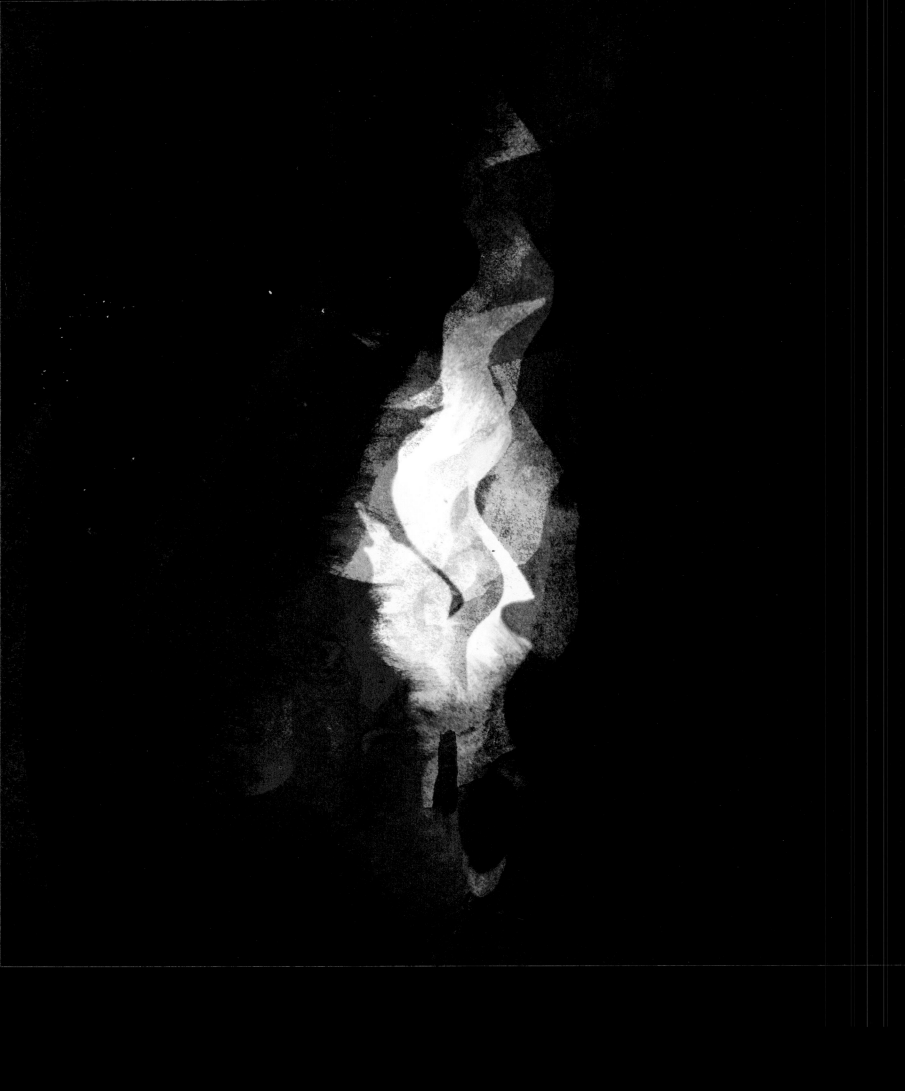

CHAPTER IV

KEEPING CHRISTMAS

FAMILIES HAVE A WAY OF establishing traditions over the years as

a means to celebrate Christmas. The same is true for the church. Over

the centuries, various traditions have come about as a means to keep

Christmas, to celebrate it as a time of reflection on the meaning of the

birth of Christ. Two traditions in particular are the Festival of Nine Carols

and Lessons, and Advent and the Advent Wreath.

NINE LESSONS & CAROLS

or the Christmas Eve service of 1880, E. W. Benson, who would become the archbishop of Canterbury, drew up an order of worship around nine Scripture readings and nine Christmas carols. Ever since, the Nine Lessons and Carols has been a meaningful service for many on Christmas Eve. The most famous version is broadcast annually as it takes place in the breathtaking cathedral of King's College, Cambridge.

The Nine Lessons and Carols, however, does not need to be exclusively sung by renowned cathedral choirs. This format for worship may be used by families wishing to celebrate the whole story of Christmas. Families with young children might want to better ensure a merry celebration by singing only the first verse of the carols. Below is the order from the service at the King's College Cathedral, utilizing a number of medieval carols. These hymns are set at a rather high degree of difficulty—especially if you forgo the English translation for the Latin original. That would be for the diehards. Others may prefer to use different hymns that prove more suitable.

I

Genesis 3:8–15, 17–19

"Remember, O Thou Man"

"Adam Lay Bounden"

II

Genesis 22:15–18

"Angels from the Realms of Glory"

"In Dulci Jubilo"

III

Isaiah 9:2, 6–7

"Nowell Sing We Now All and Some"

"Unto Us Is Born a Son"

IV

Isaiah 11:1–3a, 4a, 6–9

"The Lamb"

"A Spotless Rose is Blowing"

V

Luke 1:26–35, 38

"I Sing of a Maiden"

"The Night When She First Gave Birth"

VI

Luke 2:1, 3–7

"Sweet Baby, Sleep! What Ails My Dear?"

"What Sweeter Music Can We Bring"

VII

Luke 2:8–16

"Infant Holy, Infant Lowly"

"God Rest You Merry, Gentlemen"

VIII

Matthew 2:1–12

"Illuminare Jerusalem"

"Glory, Alleluia to the Christ Child"

IX

John 1:1–14

"O Come, All Ye Faithful"

"In Christ Alone"

CONCLUSION

"Hark! The Herald Angels Sing"

All praise, eternal Son,
to Thee, Whose advent sets
Thy people free.

—Ambrose of Milan

ADVENT

he word advent simply means coming. The Advent season, sometimes called simply Advent, refers to the time that leads up to the coming of Christ at Christmas. The church has traditionally set aside the four Sundays before Christmas as the season of Advent. Sometimes people use Advent Wreaths and candles in the celebration. Below is an order of prayers and readings for the four Sundays in Advent and for Christmas Eve.

The

First

Sunday

in

Advent

PRAYER

Almighty God, give us grace that we may put away the works of darkness and put on the armor of light now in the time of this mortal life, in which Your Son Jesus Christ came to visit us in great humility; that in the last day, when He will come again in His glorious majesty to judge both the living and the dead, we may rise to the life immortal, through Him who lives and reigns with You and the Holy Spirit, now and ever. Amen.

The first Sunday readings remind us of the promise of the Savior in the writings of the Old Testament prophets.

ISAIAH 9:2–7

READER 1:   The people walking in darkness have seen a great light; on those living in the land of the shadow of death a light has dawned. For to us a child is born, to us a son is given, and the government will be on His shoulders.

READER 2:   And He will be called Wonderful Counselor, Mighty God, Everlasting Father, Prince of Peace. Of the increase of His government and peace there will be no end. He will reign on David's throne and over His kingdom, establishing and upholding it with justice and righteousness from that time on and forever.

FAMILY: The zeal of the Lord Almighty will accomplish this.

The

Second

Sunday

in

Advent

PRAYER

Blessed Lord, who has caused all the Holy Scriptures to be written for our learning, grant that we may in such wise hear them, read, mark, learn, and inwardly digest them, that by patience and comfort of Your holy Word, we may embrace, and ever hold fast, the blessed hope of everlasting life, which You have given us in our Savior Jesus Christ. Amen.

The second Sunday readings remind us of how Christ came in humility—to an ordinary place, in a stable of animals, among an ordinary people. This is a time to remember how Christ fully identifies with humanity in the incarnation.

MICAH 5:2-5

READER 1: But you, Bethlehem Ephrathah, though you are small among the clans of Judah, out of you will come for Me one who will be ruler over Israel, whose origins are from of old, from ancient times.

READER 2: Therefore Israel will be abandoned until the time when she who is in labor gives birth and the rest of his brothers return to join the Israelites.

READER 1: He will stand and shepherd His flock in the strength of the Lord, in the majesty of the name of the Lord His God.

READER 2: And they will live securely, for then His greatness will reach to the ends of the earth.

FAMILY: And He will be their peace.

The Third Sunday in Advent

PRAYER

O Lord Jesus Christ, who at Your first coming sent Your messenger to prepare Your way, grant that the ministers and stewards of Your mysteries may likewise so prepare and make ready Your way, by turning the hearts of the disobedient to the wisdom of the just, that at Your second coming to judge the world we may be found an acceptable people in Your sight, who lives and reigns with the Father and the Holy Spirit ever, one God, world without end. Amen.

The third Sunday readings remind us of the shepherds, the first witnesses to Jesus. They also model for us how we should respond to Christ. The shepherds both told others about Christ and offered praise and thanksgiving to God for Christ. So should we.

LUKE 2:17–20

READER 1:   When they had seen Him, they spread the word concerning what had been told them about this child, and all who heard it were amazed at what the shepherds said to them.

READER 2:   But Mary treasured up all these things and pondered them in her heart.

FAMILY: The shepherds returned, glorifying and praising God for all the things they had heard and seen, which were just as they had been told.

The

Fourth

Sunday

in

Advent

PRAYER

O Lord, raise up, we pray, Your power, and come among us, and with great might succor us, that whereas, through our sins and wickedness, we are sore let and hindered in running the race that is set before us, Your bountiful grace and mercy may help and deliver us, through the satisfaction of Your Son our Lord, to whom, with You and the Holy Ghost, be honor and glory, world without end. Amen.

The fourth Sunday readings remind us of the angels. Angels proclaimed the first coming of Christ to the shepherds on the hillside. One day they will proclaim His second coming. At that time, the whole universe will hear it.

REVELATION 7:9–12

READER 1: After this I looked and there before me was a great multitude that no one could count, from every nation, tribe, people and language, standing before the throne and in front of the Lamb. They were wearing white robes and were holding palm branches in their hands. And they cried out in a loud voice:

FAMILY: "Salvation belongs to our God, who sits on the throne, and to the Lamb."

READER 2: All the angels were standing around the throne and around the elders and the four living creatures. They fell down on their faces before the throne and worshiped God, saying:

FAMILY: "Amen! Praise and glory and wisdom and thanks and honor and power and strength be to our God for ever and ever. Amen!"

Christmas

Eve

PRAYER

Almighty God, who has given us Your only begotten Son to take our nature upon Him, and as at this time to be born of a pure virgin, grant that we being regenerate, and made Your children by adoption and grace, may daily be renewed by Your Holy Spirit, through the same our Lord Jesus Christ, who lives and reigns with You and the same Spirit ever, one God, world without end. Amen.

The Christmas Eve readings remind us that the birth of Christ is not only at the center of Christmas, but that His birth, life, death, and resurrection are at the center of the Bible, the center of God's plan of redemption, and the center of all human history. Christ's incarnation, from the cradle to the cross and on to the empty tomb, is the great pivot point for all of history and all of God's plan for His creation.

JOHN 1:1–5, 9

READER 1:   In the beginning was the Word, and the Word was with God, and the Word was God. He was with God in the beginning.

READER 2:   Through Him all things were made; without Him nothing was made that has been made. In Him was life, and that life was the light of men. The light shines in the darkness, but the darkness has not understood it.

FAMILY: The true light that gives light to every man was coming into the world.

CHAPTER V

CHRISTMAS MEMORIES

FAMILIES DEVELOP traditions over the years

that lead to cherished memories of Christmas.

Use these pages to record your family traditions,

stories, and memories for generations to come.

Family Traditions

FAMILY TRADITIONS

FAMILY TRADITIONS

SOURCES

p. 17, "The English brought a soccer ball ... " Kurt Zehmisch, cited in Stanley Weintraub, *Silent Night: The Story of the World War I Christmas Truce* (New York: The Free Press, 2002) 105.

p. 18, "In the Christian story ... " C. S. Lewis, *Miracles* (New York: MacMillan, 1960) 111.

p. 21, "To perceive Christmas ... " E. B. White, *The New Yorker*, December 24, 1949.

p. 22, "Jesus, Lord, we look ... " Charles Wesley, "Jesus, Lord, We Look to Thee," 1749.

p. 24, "What human being could know ... " Augustine, "Sermon on the Nativity" in *The Fathers of the Church: Saint Augustine on the Liturgical Seasons*, Mary Sarah Muldowney (Washington D.C.: The Catholic University Press of America, 1984) 39.

p. 25, "Infinite and an infant ... " Charles Haddon Spurgeon, "The Condescension of Christ," September 13, 1857, http://www.spurgeon.org/sermons/0151.htm.

p. 26, "Mary was not chosen ... " Dietrich Bonhoeffer, "Sermon on Luke 1:46-55, December 17, 1933," cited in *Dietrich Bonhoeffer Works*, Volume 13, edited by Keith Clements (Minneapolis: Fortress Press, 2007) 343.

p. 29, "Celebrating Advent means ... " Dietrich Bonhoeffer, "Waiting at the Door," *The Collected Sermons of Dietrich Bonhoeffer*, Isabel Best, Ed. (Minneapolis: Fortress Press, 2012) 8.

p. 30, "I heard the bells on Christmas day ... " Henry Wadsworth Longfellow, "Christmas Bells," 1864.

p. 33, "The Shepherds sing ... " George Herbert, "Christmas," *George Herbert: Poems* (New York: Knopf/Everyman's Library, 2004) 85.

p. 34, "This helpless baby ... " SJN.

SOURCES

p. 39-40, "What does it mean ... " and following quotations, Dietrich Bonhoeffer, "Sermon on Luke 1:46-55, December 17, 1933," cited in *Dietrich Bonhoeffer Works*, Volume 13, edited by Keith Clements (Minneapolis: Fortress Press, 2007) 345-347.

p. 44, "O Come, O Come, Emmanuel" Latin hymn, "Veni, Veni, Emmanuel," c. 8th Century; English Translation by John Mason Neale and Henry Sloane Coffin, c. 1850.

p. 48, "A very singular thing is this ... " Charles Haddon Spurgeon, "The Incarnation and Birth of Christ," December 23, 1855, http://www.spurgeon.org/sermons/0057.htm.

p. 52, "Mary Had a Baby" Traditional African American Spiritual, Source unknown.

p. 54-55, "The Son of God did not want ... " Martin Luther, Festival of the Epiphany, 1526, cited in Paul Althaus, *The Theology of Martin Luther* (Fortress Press, 1966) 187.

p. 59, "O Little Town of Bethlehem," Philips Brooks, 1868.

p. 60, "Therefore the Word of God," Leo the Great, "Sermon XXI, On the Feast of the Nativity, I" *The Nicene and Post-Nicene Fathers*, Second Series, Volume XIII (Grand Rapids: Eerdmans, 1997 [reprint]) 129.

p. 66, "How shall I describe ... " John Chrysostom, "Christmas Morning," 386, in *The Sunday Sermons of the Great Fathers* (Swedesboro, NJ: The Preservation Press, 1996) 11.

p. 70, "Awake, mankind ... " Augustine, "On the Mystery of the Incarnation" (Sermon 185) in *Augustine: Major Writings*, Benedict J. Groeschel, Ed. (Indiana: Crossroad, 1995) 69.

p. 72, "The inn was full ... " Martin Luther, in *Martin Luther's Christmas Book*, Roland Bainton, Ed. (Philadelphia: Westminster Press, 1948) 29.

p. 74-75, "On the night Jesus ... " R. C. Sproul, *The Glory of Christ* (Carol Stream, IL: Tyndale House, 1990) 16-17.

SOURCES

p. 77, "Behold here what the Gospel … " Martin Luther, "The Birth of Jesus" in *Through the Year with Martin Luther: A Selection of Sermons Celebrating the Feasts and Seasons of the Christian Year* (Peabody, MA: Hendrickson, 2007) 108.

p. 78, "Silent Night," "Stille Nacht, Heilege Nacht," Joseph Mohr, 1818, English translation by John Freeman Young, c. 1850.

p. 83, "What is the Connection … " John Piper, "The Word Became Flesh," December 24, 1989, http://www.desiringgod.org/resource-library/sermons/the-word-became-flesh.

p. 86, "O Come, All Ye faithful … " "Adeste Fidelis," credited to John Francis Wade, 1751.

p. 90, "We have nearly arrived … " Charles Haddon Spurgeon, "Good Cheer for Christmas," December 20, 1868, http://www.iclnet.org/pub/resources/text/history/spurgeon/web/ss-0019.html.

p. 92, "Justified by faith … " Augustine, "On the Mystery of the Incarnation" (Sermon 185) in *Augustine: Major Writings*, Benedict J. Groeschel, Ed. (Indiana: Crossroad, 1995) 70.

p. 96, "This is the month … " John Milton, "On the Morning of Christ's Nativity" (1629) *The Complete Poems of John Milton in English: Harvard Classics*, Millennium Edition, Charles W. Eliot, ed. (Norwalk, CT: Easton Press, 1993) 7.

p. 101, "The Birthday of the Lord … " Leo the Great, "On the Feast of the Nativity, VI," *The Nicene and Post-Nicene Fathers*, Second Series, Volume XIII (Grand Rapids: Eerdmans, 1997 [reprint]) 138.

p. 104–105, "Go Tell It on a Mountain," Traditional African American Spiritual, Source unknown.

p. 109, On E. W. Benson and The Nine Lessons and Carols, see http://www.kings.cam.ac.uk/events/chapel-services/nine-lessons/history.html.

p. 116–125, "The First Sunday in Advent … " *The Collects of the Book of Common Prayer*, The Church Hymnal Corporation, New York

ABOUT THE AUTHOR

STEPHEN J. NICHOLS is president of Reformation Bible College. He also sits on the board of directors of Ligonier Academy of Biblical and Theological Studies, serves as Chief Academic Officer and teaching fellow for Ligonier Ministries, and is an adjunct professor at Reformed Theological Seminary. He holds a PhD from Westminster Theological Seminary.

He has written seventeen books, including *The Reformation: How a Monk and a Mallet Changed the World*; *Welcome to the Story: Reading, Loving, and Living God's Word*; and *Jesus Made in America: A Cultural History from the Puritans to "The Passion of the Christ."* He is also the teacher on the audio/video series *Reformation Profiles*, produced by Ligonier Ministries and is also host of the weekly podcast, 5 *Minutes in Church History*.

Dr. Nichols lives in Central Florida with his wife, Heidi, and their three children.